Fort Sumter

Charles W. Maynard

The Rosen Publishing Group's
PowerKids Press™
New York

For Allison, John, Almon, and Martha

Published in 2002 by The Rosen Publishing Group, Inc.
29 East 21st Street, New York, NY 10010

First Edition

Book Design: Michael Caroleo

Project Editor: Kathy Campbell

Photo Credits: pp. 4 (map and Fort Moultrie woodcut), 7 (fort plans), 8 (Major Anderson), 11 (Fort Sumter), 16 (all) © North Wind Pictures; pp. 4 (William Moultrie), 12, 19 © CORBIS; p. 7 (arial view) © William A. Bake/CORBIS; pp. 8 (Anderson occupies fort), 15 (Confederate soldiers), 20 © Bettmann/CORBIS; p. 8 (Fort Johnson) © Medford Historical Society Collection/CORBIS; p. 11 (Confederate soldiers) © Archive Photos; pp. 15 (cannon), 18 (cannon) © Kevin Fleming/CORBIS.

Maynard, Charles W. (Charles William), 1955–
Fort Sumter/Charles W. Maynard.—1st. ed.
p. cm.— (Famous forts throughout American history)
Includes index.
ISBN 0-8239-5840-X
1. Fort Sumter (Charleston, S.C.)—Siege, 1861—Juvenile literature. 2. Charleston (S.C.)—History—Civil War, 1861–1865—Juvenile literature. 3. Fort Sumter (Charleston, S.C.)—History—Juvenile literature. 4. Charleston (S.C.)—Buildings, structures, etc.—Juvenile literature. [1. Fort Sumter (Charleston, S.C.)—Siege, 1861.] I. Title.
E471.1 .M39 2002
973.7′3′09757915—dc21
00-012794

Manufactured in the United States of America

Contents

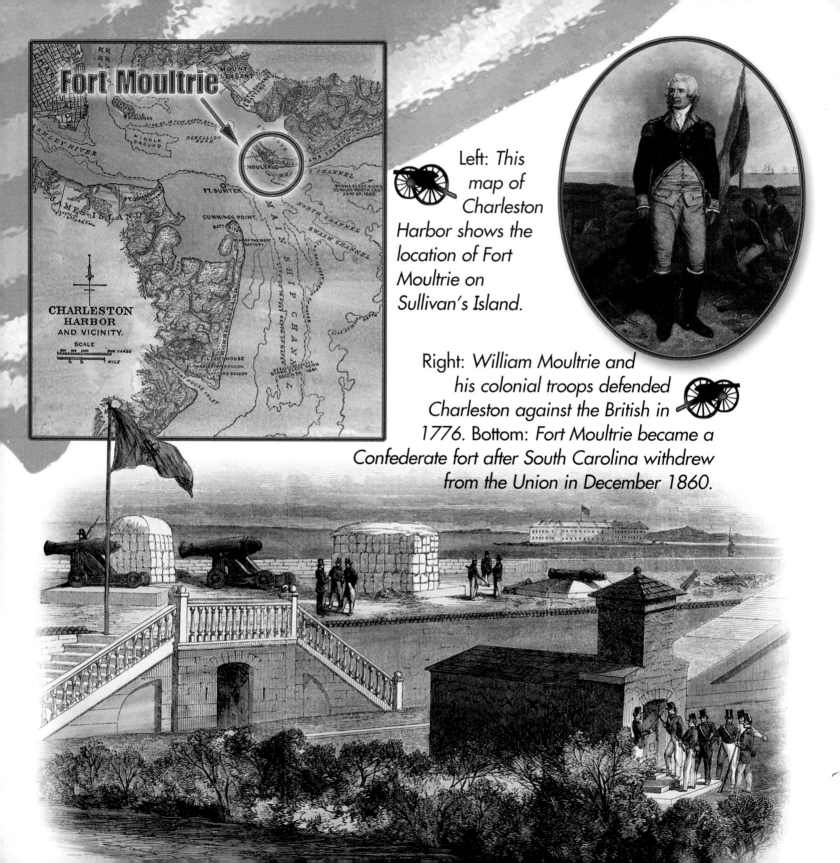

Fort Moultrie

CHARLESTON HARBOR AND VICINITY.
SCALE

Left: *This map of Charleston Harbor shows the location of Fort Moultrie on Sullivan's Island.*

Right: *William Moultrie and his colonial troops defended Charleston against the British in 1776.* Bottom: *Fort Moultrie became a Confederate fort after South Carolina withdrew from the Union in December 1860.*

Charleston Harbor

Charleston, South Carolina, is one of the most important seaports of the southeastern United States. Because of shallow water, ships enter the harbor through a narrow **channel**. During the **Revolutionary War**, Americans built a small fort on Sullivan's Island to protect Charleston Harbor. The **patriots** poured sand between two walls of palmetto wood to make Fort Moultrie. The fort was named for its commander, William Moultrie.

On June 28, 1776, nine British warships under the command of Admiral Sir Peter Parker attacked the fort. The **shot** from the British **cannons** did not harm the wooden fort. The Americans kept firing until the British ships left.

After the Revolutionary War, the little fort fell apart. The young United States built a new Fort Moultrie in 1798, in the same place. The five-sided fort had earth and timber walls 17 feet (5 m) high. A hurricane destroyed it in 1804. A third Fort Moultrie, made of brick and sand, replaced the earlier forts in 1811.

Building Fort Sumter

To better protect Charleston, the U.S. Army decided to build other forts besides Fort Moultrie around the harbor. In 1827 and 1828, army **engineers** planned a new fort for a shallow place in the harbor. Men began to work on the new fort in 1829, by building a small island with the stone blocks they had brought in by ship. On the stone, the men built a five-sided brick fort with walls 5 feet (1.5 m) thick and 50 feet (15.2 m) tall. On four of the walls, two levels with guns could **defend** the harbor and the fort. Soldiers lived in three buildings along the inside walls of the fort. The buildings faced the parade ground, which was used for drills.

In December 1860, after 32 years of construction, the fort still was not finished. Only 15 guns of the 135 guns planned for the fort were in place. The army named the fort for General Thomas Sumter, a South Carolinian who fought in the Revolutionary War.

Top: *Planners based the structure of Fort Sumter on the pentagon, a five-sided shape.*

Bottom: *Today people can take a tour boat from Charleston to visit Fort Sumter.*

SCALE OF FEET
50   100

N

DERRICK   HOT SHOT FURNACE
SPLINTER PROOF
PILE OF SHOT FURNACES
WINCH
ARRANGED AS MORTARS
10 INCHER ARRANGED AS MORTARS TO FIRE INTO CITY
FLAG STAFF
TO FIRE ON MORRIS
PILE OF SHOT & SHELL
10"-SHOT ON SKIDS
SHELL BIN
BARRACKS
BARRACKS
SHELL BIN
PILE OF RATS & RUBBISH (SERVING AS TRAVERSE)
LANTERN (ELEVATED ON TRESTLES)
SPLINTER PROOF
TRAVERSE
SP PROOF TRAVERSE
BAND ROOMS   (HOSPITAL)
ESPLANADE   SALLY-PORT   ESPLANADE
WHARF

Preparing for War

Throughout the early 1800s, people disagreed over **slavery**. Some people thought it was wrong to own slaves. Others thought slavery was right. After Abraham Lincoln, who was against slavery, was elected president in 1860, some southern states decided not to be a part of the United States anymore. Eleven states, including South Carolina, **seceded** from the nation and became the **Confederate States of America**. When these states began to secede, U.S. soldiers led by Major Robert Anderson climbed into boats in the middle of the night of December 26, 1860, and crossed the water from Fort Moultrie to the unfinished Fort Sumter. Anderson believed he could better defend Charleston from there. The people of Charleston, though, were angry at what they considered to be an act of **aggression**. Confederate soldiers took control of Castle Pinckney, Fort Moultrie, and Fort Johnson, on December 27, 1860.

Top Left: *Major Robert Anderson commanded the forts in Charleston Harbor.* Top Right: *These are cannonballs at Fort Johnson.* Bottom: *Anderson rowed to Fort Sumter to defend Charleston against the Confederates.*

Attack on Fort Sumter

For four months, Major Robert Anderson and his men prepared Fort Sumter for battle. The Confederate soldiers moved into Fort Moultrie and other forts around Charleston Harbor. In the spring of 1861, following the wishes of the Confederate **government**, messengers went by boat to Fort Sumter to speak to Major Anderson. They asked him to **surrender** the fort, but he refused.

After a second warning in the early morning hours of April 12, 1861, the Confederates began firing on Fort Sumter. These shots began the **Civil War**. The attack on the fort lasted for 34 hours. Despite some return fire from Major Anderson, the Union soldiers were forced to surrender. During the attack, soldiers of each army suffered wounds, but none died.

Top: *The Confederates who took over the other three forts in Charleston Harbor open fire on Fort Sumter on April 12. Bottom: The Confederates at Fort Moultrie fired at Fort Sumter with cannons.*

A Confederate Fort

Major Anderson lowered the U.S. flag at noon on April 14, 1861, and removed his men from Fort Sumter. When the Confederate army took over the fort, they repaired and improved it. Soldiers strengthened the walls by adding sand and large, bound packages of cotton, called bales, to the rooms inside the fort walls.

Fort Sumter's new garrison, the group of soldiers stationed at the fort, brought more guns to better protect the harbor entrance. Because the Confederates controlled Fort Sumter, Fort Moultrie, and other forts around the harbor, the people of Charleston did not fear a Union attack. For the next few years while the Union and Confederacy fought the Civil War, Confederates lived, worked, and fought in Fort Sumter.

Confederate soldiers stand inside Fort Sumter on April 15, 1861, the day after Major Anderson surrendered the fort. The flag on the fort's pole is the Stars and Bars, the first flag of the Confederate States of America.

13

Life at Fort Sumter

Confederate soldiers worked hard to make Fort Sumter stronger. The 500 soldiers who lived in the fort drilled on the parade ground and fixed the **barracks**. Boats brought supplies to the stone dock. After unloading, soldiers carried food, **gunpowder**, and shot into the fort through the **sally port** in the **gorge wall**. The island fort was like a small town with a bakery, a furnace for heating iron, a fire engine, a shoe factory, and a machine for making fresh water from salt water.

Many days and months passed with no fighting, but the soldiers stayed ready. Sometimes they practiced firing some of the fort's 95 guns. During battles the soldiers found shelter in the thick walls of Fort Sumter. The Union army and navy could not get past the guns of Fort Sumter or the other forts to take the city of Charleston.

*Top: Fort Sumter's 95 guns (one of which is seen here) and 500 Confederate soldiers held back the Union forces from 1861 to 1865.
Bottom: Confederate soldiers watch over Battery Beauregard (a group of guns) near Fort Sumter in 1864. Brigadier General P. G. T. Beauregard commanded the Confederate forces around Charleston in 1861.*

Top: *The U.S. flag pictured here is the one that Major Robert Anderson lowered when Union troops surrendered Fort Sumter in April 1861. Anderson brought back the flag in April 1865 when the Union regained the fort.*

Bottom: *Some of the Union navy's ironclad ships, including the Weehawken and Passaic, bombard the Confederate-held Fort Sumter in 1863.*

The Union Retakes Fort Sumter

The Union first tried to retake Fort Sumter by attacking it with **ironclad ships** in April 1863. The Confederates stopped the Union ships with cannon fire from Fort Sumter and Fort Moultrie. In the 2½-hour-long battle, the Confederates fired more than 2,000 shots while the Union gunboats returned only 154 shots. Next the Union tried to take Fort Sumter by land and sea. The army fired on the fort from nearby Morris Island. On April 17, 1863, the **bombardment** began with more than 1,000 shells fired on the first day. The Union guns shattered its walls, but the fort with its defenders refused to fall. For 22 months, Fort Sumter withstood the Union guns that fired more than 7 million pounds (3.2 million kg) of metal. Finally, on February 17, 1865, the Confederates left Fort Sumter after a large Union army came from Savannah, Georgia. On April 14, 1865, Major Robert Anderson returned to raise the Union flag over the ruined fort.

After the Civil War

In 1865, the Union army repaired the fort and added a lighthouse to one of its corners. From 1876 to 1897, Fort Sumter held no soldiers but served only as a lighthouse station at the harbor's entrance. The gun platforms rotted and the guns rusted. With the beginning of the Spanish-American War in 1898, the U.S. Army returned to build **Battery** Huger inside the old fort. Two long-range rifles completed the battery the next year. These guns were never fired in battle.

The army once again manned the fort to guard the harbor entrance during World War I (1914–18).

This view of flags and a cannon can be seen today at Fort Sumter.

During World War II (1939–45), two antiaircraft guns replaced the rifles in Battery Huger, but the small fort faced no attacks. The U.S. government made Fort Sumter a national **monument** in 1948.

This photograph from the early 1860s shows the lighthouse at Fort Sumter.

Timeline

1776   Fort Moultrie is built on Sullivan's Island.

1798   A second Fort Moultrie is built.

1804   Fort Moultrie is ruined by a hurricane.

1811   A third Fort Moultrie is built.

1827-1828   Plans are drawn for Fort Sumter.

1829   Construction begins on Fort Sumter.

1860   On December 20, South Carolina secedes from the Union; on December 26, U.S. Army Major Robert Anderson removes his men from Fort Moultrie to Fort Sumter.

1861   On April 12-13, the Confederates bombard Fort Sumter; on April 14, Major Anderson surrenders and leaves Fort Sumter. Confederates move into the fort.

1863   On April 7, Union gunboats attack Fort Sumter; on April 17, the Union army and navy start to bombard Fort Sumter.

1865   On February 17, Confederates leave Fort Sumter to Union troops; on April 14, Major Anderson raises the flag at Fort Sumter.

1898   Battery Huger is built at Fort Sumter.

1943   Antiaircraft guns are placed in Battery Huger.

1948   Fort Sumter becomes a national monument.

A History of Guarding Charleston Harbor

Throughout its history, whether as a fort or a lighthouse, Fort Sumter stood guard over the entrance to Charleston Harbor. Fort Sumter received the first shots of the Civil War. It later **symbolized** the Confederate cause. Fort Sumter now reminds us of the Civil War, the war that tore apart the United States.

This painting by Conrad Wise Chapman shows Fort Sumter at sunset after the Union bombardment of 1863.

Visiting Fort Sumter Today

Today visitors ride a boat from the city of Charleston through Charleston Harbor and out to Fort Sumter for a walking tour of the rebuilt brick fort. Many guns from the Civil War point through the thick walls toward the harbor. Copies of the Union and Confederate flags flap in the sea breeze high above the parade ground. Three cannonballs from the Civil War battles still are stuck in the brick walls. Battery Huger sits amid the older Civil War fort.

Visitors can walk all over the 2½ acres (1 ha) of the fort that silently guards Charleston Harbor. The National Park Service also cares for Fort Moultrie on Sullivan's Island. National Park rangers give talks and demonstrations about life and battles at Fort Sumter. Visitors can learn about American history, from the Revolutionary War to World War II.

Glossary

aggression (uh-GREH-shin) Mean behavior or an attack on someone or something.

barracks (BAR-iks) Buildings where soldiers live.

battery (BA-tuh-ree) A group of guns.

bombardment (bom-BARD-mint) An attack with large firearms, such as cannons.

cannons (KA-nunz) Large guns with a smooth bore barrel.

channel (CHA-nuhl) The deepest part of a harbor.

Civil War (SIH-vul WOR) A war between two sides within one country. The American Civil War was fought in the United States between the Union (northern states) and the Confederates (southern states) from 1861 to 1865.

Confederate States of America (con-FEH-duh-ret STAYTZ UV uh-MER-ih-kuh) A group of 11 southern states that declared themselves separate from the United States in 1860–61.

defend (dih-FEND) To protect from attack or harm.

engineers (en-jih-NEERZ) People who are experts at planning and building engines, machines, roads, bridges, forts, and canals.

gorge wall (GORJ WAL) A long, narrow, straight wall at a fort.

government (GUH-vern-mint) The people who make laws and run a state or country.

gunpowder (GUN-pow-dur) A black powder that explodes in a gun and moves the bullet.

ironclad ships (EYE-urn-klad SHIPS) Ships covered with iron or steel to protect them from shot.

monument (MAHN-yoo-mint) Something built to honor a person or an event.

patriots (PAY-tree-uhtz) People who love and defend their country.

Revolutionary War (reh-vuh-LOO-shuh-nayr-ee WOR) The war American colonists fought from 1775 to 1783 to win independence from England.

sally port (SA-lee PORT) The entrance to a fort, with two sets of large doors.

seceded (sih-SEED-ed) To have withdrawn from a group or country.

shot (SHAHT) Metal objects fired from weapons such as guns and cannons.

slavery (SLAY-vuh-ree) The system of one person owning another.

surrender (suh-REN-der) To give up.

symbolized (SIM-buh-lyzd) To have stood for something important.

Index

Web Sites

To learn more about Fort Sumter, check out these Web sites:

www.ccpl.org/ccl/sumtertour.html
www.civilwarhome.com/ftsumter.htm
www.tulane.edu/~latner/CrisisMain.html